Tell Me Why

WHY?

I Have a Belly Button

Jennifer Colby

Published in the United States of America by Cherry Lake Publishing
Ann Arbor, Michigan
www.cherrylakepublishing.com

Content Adviser: Charisse Gencyuz, M.D., Clinical Instructor, Department of Internal Medicine,
University of Michigan
Reading Adviser: Marla Conn, ReadAbility, Inc

Photo Credits: © Donald Bowers Photography/Shutterstock Images, cover, 1, 15; © Phon Promwisate/
Shutterstock Images, cover, 1, 5; © Claudia Paulussen/Shutterstock Images, 7; © Karen Grigoryan/
Shutterstock Images, 9; © Monkey Business Images/Shutterstock Images, 11; © mmutlu/Shutterstock
Images, 13; © Bildagentur Zoonar GmbH/Shutterstock Images, cover, 1, 17; © Amnartk/Shutterstock
Images, 19; © Golden Pixels LLC/Shutterstock Images, 21

Library of Congress Cataloging-in-Publication Data

Colby, Jennifer, 1971- author.
 I have a belly button / Jennifer Colby.
    pages cm. — (Tell me why)
 Summary: "Young children are naturally curious about themselves. I Have a Belly Button offers answers
to their most compelling questions about their bellybuttons. Age-appropriate explanations and appealing
photos encourage readers to continue their quest for knowledge. Additional text features and search
tools, including a glossary and an index, help students locate information and learn new words."—
Provided by publisher.
 Audience: Ages 6—10
 Audience: K to grade 3
 Includes bibliographical references and index.
 ISBN 978-1-63362-612-6 (hardcover) — ISBN 978-1-63362-702-4 (pbk.) —
ISBN 978-1-63362-792-5 (pdf) — ISBN 978-1-63362-882-3 (ebook)
 1. Navel—Juvenile literature. 2. Umbilical cord—Juvenile literature. 3. Childbirth—Juvenile literature.
4. Pregnancy—Juvenile literature. I. Title. II. Series: Tell me why (Cherry Lake Publishing)

QM543.C65 2016
612.6'3—dc23

                            2014049836

Cherry Lake Publishing would like to acknowledge the work of the Partnership for 21st Century Skills.
Please visit www.p21.org for more information.

Printed in the United States of America
Corporate Graphics

Table of Contents

A New Baby in the Family

Mariah's new little brother just came home from the hospital. She helped her mother change the baby's diaper.

"What is that thing on his tummy?" she asked. "Is he okay?"

Mariah's mom assured her that her brother was just fine. "All babies have this when they are born," her mom said. "It's actually an **umbilical cord** stump."

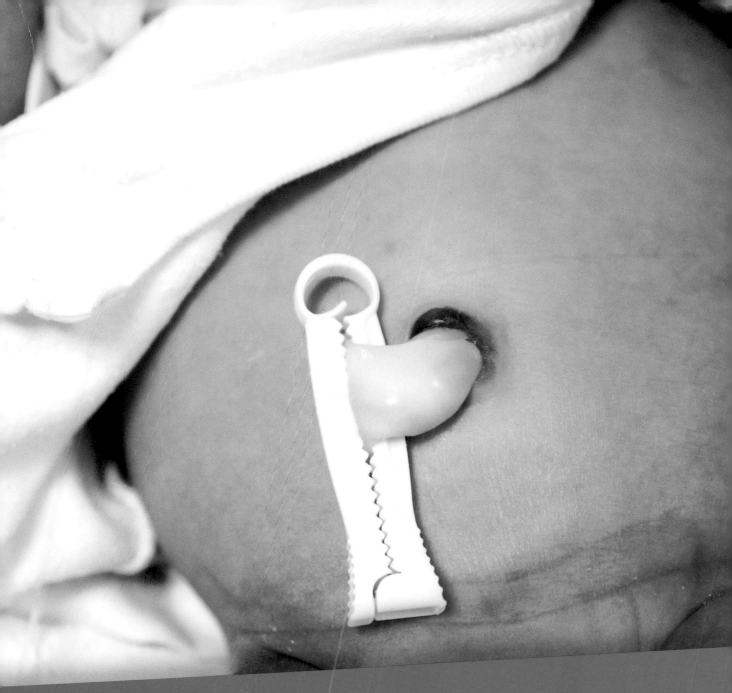

All newborn babies have an umbilical cord stump.

Mariah was confused. "A cord stump? What's that?"

"It was part of how your brother lived inside me," Mom said. "The cord used to be longer. It connected us. Now this is what's left. It will fall off soon. All belly buttons start out this way!"

"You mean just like mine?" Mariah asked.

"Yes," Mom said, "just like yours."

All people have belly buttons.

A baby is born with a long cord attached to the belly. The doctor delivers the baby and cuts the cord. The baby does not feel any pain. The cord stump is what is left. This will fall off in one to two weeks. The belly button is what is left in that space.

Once a baby is born, the belly button is not used for anything.

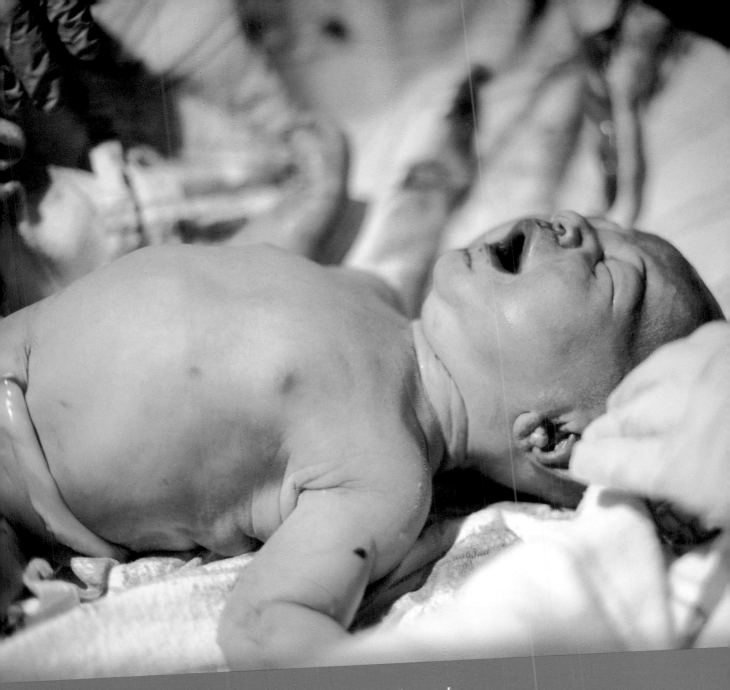

When a baby is born, the doctor needs to cut the cord.

The Cord's Job

A baby growing inside its mother cannot eat food or breathe.

That's where the umbilical cord comes in. It is attached to the **placenta** inside the mother's **womb**. Your belly button marks the spot where the placenta was attached when you were a baby!

The umbilical cord looks like a twisted rope. It grows longer during the **pregnancy**.

Most umbilical cords grow to be about 20 inches (51 centimeters) long.

MAKE A GUESS!

A belly button is also called a navel. Some oranges are called navel oranges. Why do you think they are called that?

The umbilical cord makes it possible for a baby to grow while inside its mother.

11

The umbilical cord carries **nutrients** and oxygen from the mother to the baby. It also takes **waste** away from the baby.

A **newborn** baby can drink milk and get rid of waste on its own. The baby does not need an umbilical cord anymore.

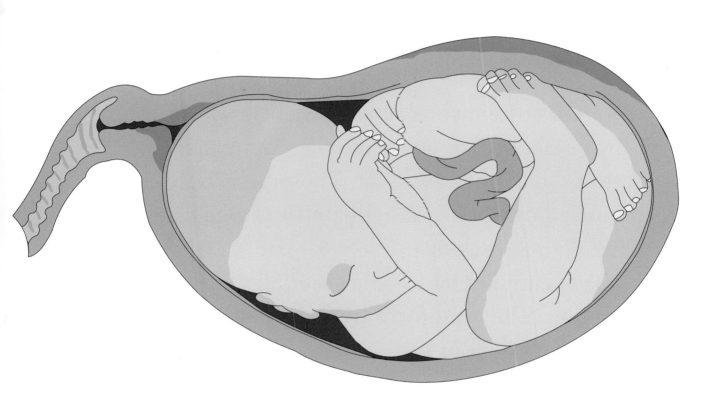

An umbilical cord connects an unborn baby to the placenta inside the mother's womb.

Innies and Outies

Parents often wonder what their newborn baby's belly button will look like. Some belly buttons stick out a little bit. These belly buttons are called outies. Most belly buttons are innies. They do not stick out.

No one knows why some are innies and some are outies. They just form that way naturally. How the cord is cut has nothing to do with it.

Most people have "innies." But some people have "outies." Ask your friends and family if they have an innie or an outie.

No two belly buttons are exactly the same, even for twins.

Your belly button is your very first scar. It is the **tissue** left over from where the umbilical cord connected you to your mother. No two belly buttons are alike.

Almost every **mammal** has a belly button. (The only ones who don't are the few species of mammals that lay eggs.) Even your cat or dog has a belly button. Every mammal's belly button is located in the same place, right in the middle of the belly.

This newborn lamb still has its umbilical cord attached.

17

Taking Care of a Newborn Baby's Belly Button

The area around a newborn baby's cord stump must be kept clean and dry. Diapers often touch the cord stump area. So it is important to clean this area when a diaper is changed. The diaper should be folded below the cord stump. This helps keep the area dry.

After the stump falls off, the area should be cleaned daily. It no longer needs cleaning when the belly button has healed.

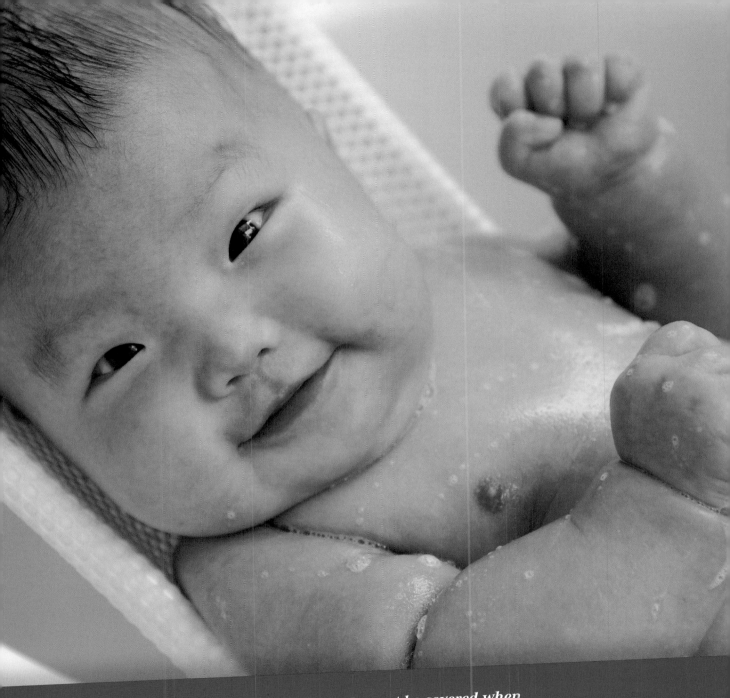

A baby's cord stump should not get wet. It must be covered when the baby is taking a bath.

Mariah's brother lost his cord stump in about 10 days. The cord stump began to dry up. Then it started to loosen from his belly. Mariah's mother kept the area clean and dry. One day, the stump fell off! Her mother found it inside his diaper.

Now Mariah can see her brother's belly button. It is an innie just like hers!

Will you be helping a grown-up with a baby? If so, ask if you can look at the brand-new belly button.

Think About It!

Humans are mammals. Almost all mammals give birth to live <u>young</u>. But the platypus and the echidna are two mammals that lay eggs instead. Go online to find out more about these fascinating creatures. Do you think they have belly buttons? Why or why not?

Ask your parents to tell you about the day you were born. Did the doctor cut the umbilical cord, or did someone else? What else do they remember about being at the hospital? Ask if they can show you any photos of you as a newborn.

Glossary

mammal (MAM-mil) a type of animal that feeds milk to its young and usually has hair or fur covering most of its skin

newborn (NOO-born) recently born

nutrients (NOO-tree-uhnts) substances that plants, animals, and people need to live and grow

placenta (pluh-SEN-tuh) the organ in mammals that forms inside the mother's uterus and nourishes the unborn baby

pregnancy (PREG-nen-see) the condition of a woman or female animal that is going to have a baby or babies

tissue (TISH-oo) the material that forms the parts in a plant or animal

umbilical cord (uhm-BIL-ih-kuhl KORD) a long, narrow tube that connects an unborn baby to the placenta of its mother

waste (WAYST) what the body does not use or need after food has been digested

womb (WOOMB) the organ in women and some female animals in which babies develop in before birth

Find Out More

Books:

Jenkins, Steve. *My First Day.* Boston: Houghton Mifflin Harcourt, 2013.

Amsel, Sheri. *The Everything KIDS' Human Body Book: All You Need to Know About Your Body Systems - From Head to Toe!* Avon, MA: Adams Media, 2012.

Web Sites:

KidsHealth—What's in Your Belly Button?
http://kidshealth.org/kid/talk/yucky/bb_inside.html
Read about the bacteria that can be found in your belly button.

KidsHealth—Why Do I Have a Belly Button?
http://kidshealth.org/kid/talk/qa/navel.html
Read about what happens right after a baby is born.

San Diego Zoo Kids—Mammals
http://kids.sandiegozoo.org/animals/mammals
Learn about the mammals of the San Diego Zoo.

Index

About the Author

Jennifer Colby lives in Michigan with her three children. They all have innies. She is a school librarian and loves to help students and teachers find the information they are looking for.